Hot Mess

poems by

J. Andersen

Finishing Line Press
Georgetown, Kentucky

Hot Mess

Copyright © 2021 by J. Andersen
ISBN 978-1-64662-648-9 First Edition
All rights reserved under International and Pan-American Copyright Conventions. No part of this book may be reproduced in any manner whatsoever without written permission from the publisher, except in the case of brief quotations embodied in critical articles and reviews.

Publisher: Leah Huete de Maines

Editor: Christen Kincaid

Cover Art: Karrah Kobus

Author Photo: Courtesy of author

Cover Design: Elizabeth Maines McCleavy

Order online: www.finishinglinepress.com
also available on amazon.com

Author inquiries and mail orders:
Finishing Line Press
PO Box 1626
Georgetown, Kentucky 40324
USA

Table of Contents

Breathing Fire 1

Wish You Were Here 3

When I Just Start Saying Fuck It 4

Guess I Learned How to Live with Myself 5

It's True That 6

What If I Told You 7

Everything You Could Ever Want is on The Other Side of Yourself 8

Untitled 9

The Story of You 10

My Vagina 11

Survival of the Fittest 12

Thanks 13

Bar Fight 14

This Thing Called Space 15

The One Time I Over-explained Myself and Now 16

When You Lose another Child 17

Confessions 18

Luminous 19

I Want ToBelieve 20

Everyday Life 21

Having a Serious Talk With Myself 22

I Lost Myself One Day 23

For anyone who feels like a hot mess

Breathing Fire

I can't say I'm the best fighter,
or the best lover or
the best partner or the best
at anything really. But
when I breathe in
my chest inflates with the fists
of the Earth. The whole
universe
trembles with one breath. It's that fragile.

It isn't like me to admit when
something is wrong but damnit
it is. There's too much going on
in the shadows
and my head grows dark
with infection as I stare
but can't see what's right
in front of me. Call it anxiety.
Call it neuroticism.
Call it whatever you want.

It's my father not telling me that he
had a heart attack two days
before Christmas or when my mother
lost her job again. It's when I was five
and I watched my brother soar into
the kitchen cabinets but he wasn't flying.
And my father breathed fire into our house.
And the thunder carried me away
as it rumbled. And the ghosts in the basement
made promises they couldn't keep.

It's when I keep thinking I'm
dreaming but I'm not. It's losing two
children and never trying again.
It's not finding the gold at the end of the rainbow.
Or when I forget to pay the electric.
Or when my daughter gets sick with the flu.
Or when I can't catch my breath.
I start gasping and cursing
everything from my flat feet to the fading sky.

Wish You Were Here

You didn't have the chance
to breathe in. Never got to watch
a soft breeze dance with the aspens.
You didn't laugh. Didn't cry.
Didn't fall and stand back up.
Didn't stare at the sun so long
you went blind. Or feel how cold
the earth is when you dig deep enough.

Never got to feel the gritty sand
or get annoyed with how it sticks
to your skin. Didn't taste snow or salt
water or hot chocolate or cheese pizza.
Didn't wonder why the stars
are always blinking or how the moon
seems to follow you everywhere you go.

When I look at the sky I wish
we were looking up together.
Still wish things could be different.
Or that the holidays weren't so damn sad
when stillness gets the best of me.
Wish I didn't have to be scared
when I am. Wish I didn't have
to admit it. Wish we had been
given a chance. Just wish you
were here, Ben. Wish you were here.

When I Just Start Saying Fuck It

Bravery is something you learn
from being broken but I'm done with being brave.
Sometimes I just want to roll around in the muck of it all.

Become one with my own bullshit. Accept it.

Take it out on a first date and try to understand it.
Maybe take it home. Sleep with it then never return its phone calls.

Because sometimes it just feels good to leave the pieces of me everywhere.
I'll burn everything in my path and keep running.
I swear I will.

Guess I Learned How to Live with Myself

Poetry taught me to be naked.

To howl at people.
To never be up front about anything
because it'll make for a great line one day.
Or a stanza depending on the situation.

There are things I can tell the world that just break me if I tell you.
I don't know why that is.

But poetry is like whispering
to a stranger. Lighting fire to my bones.
Dancing to the beat of monsters at times.
And never knowing where my
fucking keys are. Or having the same conversation
a thousand times but still not listening.

The sky keeps sending Morse code
behind you. I'm just a thunderclap
away from understanding it.
Just right there next to you but
not really. And I keep trying to
find the right way to describe
your eyes to everyone else
but you. I swear I don't know why.

It's True That

only when the earth is screaming can I feel the everything in everything.

What if I Told You?

That maybe I didn't hate myself. I just wanted to. And the stars didn't scare me. I actually believed in them. Your eyes are like rockets shooting through me and that's ok. That we wave our hearts like flags but still give into our demons.

Or that I want to marry the moon. I want to feel the earth spinning beneath me. I love being dizzy. Maybe love is real and maybe love has to crush you for you to grow and maybe love is the reason I'm still alive. That without you this land that is my body is cursed. My bones are too weak for walking anymore. I can't feel my toes most of the time.

What if I told you sometimes I like to give you the creeps. Sometimes I pretend I don't exist. It's hard to tell when I'm going to jump off the deep end again but I know it's gonna happen. I just hope you can swim. I really fucking hope.

There's nothing like hot breath against cold glass. Or drawing hearts around your name. Carving your initials into my rib cage. Feeling like I'm in high school again because I can't stop listening to Taking Back Sunday with the windows down, screaming your name in between songs so loud the whole earth trembles.

**Everything You Could Ever Want is on
The Other Side of Yourself**

This is what I tell myself
after the butterflies have left
my body. When my shelter has
been trashed. I keep telling you
I can't do this but I don't even know
what this is. Don't look at me like that.
Don't tell me the same old love stories.
Don't try to make me feel better.

I know I keep ghosting you.
I don't even know how to stop.
But I mean it when I say I need
us to last forever otherwise
I'm totally fucked. I need you
to please be gentle. Save me from myself
after all the years of telling you I don't
need to be saved. I drown
whenever you aren't here.
I don't exist outside of this
space we created.
Together.

Took too much time memorizing
every one of your crooked teeth.
The way your muscles twitch
as you sleep. Like you're dancing
with me. But you aren't.
I keep hoping you will.

Can we stare into the sun until we go blind and we'll never have to see our demons again?

The Story of You

Maybe that's just how you are.

Putting your entire being
into something and not
getting anything back.

That's what makes you so beautiful.

You are broken and somehow
always naked and slouching
slightly. You are fucking perfect.
You deserve the world even
when you don't believe it.

Every scar still healing against
your skin is your magnum opus.
Every line on your face tells
the story of you.
When you smile.
And when you don't.

My Vagina

and I have a complicated relationship.
I think she's beautiful.
        She thinks she could use some work.
The more I tell her that she's perfect
the more she pushes me away. Like she's scared.
I don't know of what but when I try to hold her
        she gets all testy.
When I try to tell her everything will be alright,
she runs.

When I'm silent she thinks something is wrong.
When I'm crying she thinks it's her fault.
        I never told her about how many cracks
there are on my heart or how every time I let her wander
she always makes the wrong decisions
but that I still love her.
        I should tell her that more often. But I don't.

Survival of the Fittest

I'm not trying
to simply survive
anymore.
I want happiness.
I want it stapled
to my forehead.
Etched into my chest.
I want to look into my own eyes
and fall madly in love.
The head over heels kind of love.
The kind people sing songs
about or dance wildly
in the streets
or get tattoos of when
they are definitely too drunk.

Thanks

      I just want to say thank you
for every time I told you I loved you
but you didn't say it back.

      And for the one time you did.
Thank you for the cigarettes and the fake
orgasms. Thank you for empty kisses
and playing video games. For giving
me a chance when you had no choice.

      For shower sex and in your parents' bed sex.
For the nights when I knew you were lying so
I'd drive by your house listening to Abbey
Road, chain smoking just to stop the shaking.

      And your car wouldn't be there.
           Even though you said you were going to bed early.
Thank you for that.

Bar Fight

One
       of us

 is leaving here

before   broken
the night
is

      through.

I
promise.

This Thing Called Space

There's a piece of me floating through this thing called space.

>Your space.
>Her space.

>What used to be left of me space.

This piece of me likes to bring attention to herself.
Sometimes somersaulting past the Milky Way.
>Sometimes haunting people she's never met.
Or people she has. It depends on the mood.
>I swear I get jealous of her. Her spirit and how it's still light.

Full of hope and flying fucks.

I'm talking how I used to be before the end of the world.
Before the two stillbirths and the flashbacks.
Not giving a fuck, shirtless and shoeless because "fuck your establishment."

This piece of me is fierce. She breathes fire when the sun sets.
She believes in things like Murphy's Law and Big Foot.
I wonder if she will ever come back or will she venture further.
Past the rivers and downtown bars and mountains and even the moon.

Will she be able to teach me things that I could never understand
like why does some love fade over time
>or how can I still put a smile on my face or

how to not be terrified of everything.

I wish she'd write more but she doesn't.
>I wish I could be her but I can't.

That One Time I Over-explained Myself and Now

I don't know what's worse:
you knowing the truth

                                        or how you said nothing back.

I guess saying nothing is saying something, though, isn't it.
Just not what I wanted
                                but definitely what I deserve.

When You Lose another Child

This is it. There is no ghost to wave to.
No one to tell me it's ok even when it's not.
I've never hated silence like this.
The moment a stranger has to look at me
and the only thing she can say is sorry.

And I don't even know what she's sorry for.
My dead child. Or that this happened to me twice.
Or that she simply has to tell me the bad news,
Or that I'm broken.

I don't know or even care anymore.
It's taken everything
just for me to be able to breathe.
And now I have to relive it all again.
Burying a baby, a name, a body, a hope,
a fucking dream.

You just don't know
how hard the bottom is
until you actually hit it.
I mean smack the ground
and bounce
back into the air,
that's how hard you fall.

Confessions

All I want is to breathe shaky
with you every morning.
Every second.
Every time things start to get a little hazy
and start to come undone.

But I've floated too far away
and you stayed glued to the ground.

Good for you.

Sometimes it's hard to remember myself.
Who I was before.
Before I was scared of the world.
Before every stranger was a threat.
Before I took you seriously.

Who knew that life really would be full
of so many broken promises
and disappointments.

I should've listened to you.

And here I am:
A disappointment.
Saying sorry when I don't know what else
to say and thinking about that time when
reality was a sheet folding in on itself in
front of us and all we could do was
watch it, hands clasped tightly
so we wouldn't lose each
other in the madness.

Luminous

Have you ever been told
that you're
glowing?

And do you remember how it felt?
I do.

Every single time (because it's only happened
three times in my life) but I remember.

The way I didn't know what to say.
But how I fell in love with myself every time.
And I wasn't just a shadow
on the moon anymore.
I was being noticed as
something more than myself.

Like being someone's favorite
bedroom wall poster.

From strangers on foreign
airport bar stools
to the chaos of bass music
shaking me apart atom by atom,
I was glowing.

Down to the security I felt in
the bed sheets as you and I held
onto the fading parts of each other,
and you said it.
I was glowing.

I didn't even know what it meant.
But I kissed you
and wanted to believe
every word that came out of your mouth.

I wanted so desperately for
you to believe every word that came out
of mine.

I Want To Believe

That my brain isn't burnt pizza,
where I still get eaten
but no one really
enjoyed it.
Maybe my feet
aren't mashed
potatoes.
Maybe that's why
I don't get anywhere.
I want to believe
the post man
isn't the devil.
And that chocolate never expires.
But I don't want
to believe
that everything means nothing.
Somewhere
in the midst of
all the bullshit
I think there's
still a chance
for me
to believe
in something.

Everyday Life

Me: I'm fine. Don't worry about me.

Also me: My daughter just asked when her dead sister was coming out of mommy's belly.
And all I could tell her is I love her. Don't worry.

Having a Serious Talk with Myself

Maybe one day you will understand
it all and maybe you won't.
And it doesn't really matter if
your questions are ever answered
when it all ends the same. Taking
that one final breath that can either
seem to echo across the entire earth
or be the hardest breath
you've ever taken.

I just hope my last words can
be something truly astounding
like how there should be marshmallows
in cocoa pebbles.

Something profound that makes no
sense to anyone unless they are upside down.

Maybe you'll get it one day.
Maybe you won't.
It really doesn't matter.

I Lost Myself One Day

walking from the bed to the fridge
and I've been looking ever since.

Behind every baby toy, every smile.
In the dryer. Under the sheets.

Sometimes I see her in the corner.
Sometimes it's when I wake up at 2:45 am
and I can't fall back sleep.

When I think I'm alone.
When I think I'm not.
It happens like that, you know.
One minute you're together.
The next you're falling apart.

Losing the parts of you
that you worked so hard on.

The ones you really loved.
Or hated. It's the same thing, really.

"She is clothed with strength and dignity; she can laugh at the days to come."
—Proverbs 31:25

J. Andersen has always been intrigued by the absurdity and uncertainty of life. In *Hot Mess* she writes about some of the tougher aspects of it, looking at life, death, love, grief, and so much more, yet finding beauty where others may not. That's what *Hot Mess* is. The bizarre and the beautiful. Just one tangled, hot mess.

J. Andersen studied Creative Writing at UCF where she graduated at the top of her class and was awarded the Most Outstanding Poet Award in 2012. Deeply involved in her local community, she helped organize the first Florida Writer's Conference at UCF, interned at *The Florida Review* for two years and often performed spoken word at local venues or on campus. She self-published a chapbook called *Tongue Anatomy* in 2012 and moved on to get a Master's Degree in Screen Writing from Full Sail University in 2019. When she's not writing feverishly, she spends her time at home with her family, working on future film projects and outreach programs, creating concept packages for businesses together, and enjoying this mad world that we live in.

www.ingramcontent.com/pod-product-compliance
Lightning Source LLC
LaVergne TN
LVHW041519070426
835507LV00012B/1682